# Études

*poems by*

# Sarah Sutro

*Finishing Line Press*
Georgetown, Kentucky

# Études

## ACKNOWLEDGMENTS

Thanks to the Goetemann Artist Residency at Rocky Neck Art Colony, inspiration for "The Light Water Carries."


Editor: Christen Kincaid

Cover Art: Sarah Sutro

Author Photo: Michael Bedford

Cover Design: Elizabeth Maines


Printed in the USA on acid-free paper.
Order online: www.finishinglinepress.com
              also available on amazon.com

Author inquiries and mail orders:
Finishing Line Press
P. O. Box 1626
Georgetown, Kentucky 40324
U. S. A.

# Table of Contents

Monarch on Orange Tree .............................................. 1

Twilight ................................................................. 2

Mercuric ................................................................ 3

Beyond Time ........................................................... 4

The Light Water Carries ............................................ 6

Snow Zen ............................................................... 10

April ..................................................................... 11

Raga ..................................................................... 13

May, Ocean ........................................................... 14

July Études ............................................................ 15

Garden of the Hesperides ......................................... 18

Sailboat 1, Sailboat 2, Man in Lime Colored Suit .............. 19

Friends .................................................................. 21

Cabbage ................................................................ 22

Success .................................................................. 24

After the Paradisal Age ............................................. 25

Mountain ............................................................... 26

*for MB*

## Monarch on Orange Tree


seemingly insulated from change
change happens anyway.
the kind we can do nothing about

recounting stories
of what was, or
might have been:

your dark-edged face,
bright eyes, mind leaning
towards infinity—
gone

black eyed susans in a blur
echinacea,
purple asters

the time it takes to absorb
someone is gone—
the time it takes to remember,
miss them,
reconcile their absence—

alone in the
garden, sorting weeds, late
flowers, Fall
afoot

monarch on orange tree
—then gone

## Twilight

blue beauty
of twilight
deep, Cimmerian blue
not night,
hovering between light
and dark moment
of diffusion,
early winter to mid
blue violet
pause
a smudge of moon in
the upper corner
of the window.
radio
plays
old spirituals,
fan spirals
twirling
on the glass:
blue grows deeper,
darker,
moon bright
except when clouds
pass

## Mercuric

golden sandals,
    hidden
among sneakers
    and high heels
light wrapping feet,
    fleet

wearing them
    I move
into myth,
    thoughts
spring up
    with each step as if
walking on a path
    of small white
flowers or red thyme,
    aromatic
and sweet

from Asia,
    one great marketplace
ripe with color,
    to Greece,
mind's eye in the starry
    air, sandy
hillside, grove of
    silver olive

walking in blossoms
    in golden sandals,
wind in my hair and
    at my feet

## Beyond Time

once bright human landscape
encoded in color
and shape bound
by pattern,
now color leaping
off canvas
in musical bands,
nearly abstract.
a visioning,
beyond time.

just the other day
I thought I glimpsed
perfection
as we drove up the mountain
and across—
    a tree, in snow,
    above a house
    its branches creating
    an actual sphere
is it possible such things exist
    or are they in my mind
    my desire to see the sphere,
    creates it
on a windy, bright late
    winter day—
    sun spinning across
    white fields
that tree—splayed
    like a broad hand
over the house,
a kind of protection.

form becomes a kind of
symbol, color
seen unexpectedly,
lightens
what we believe—

as if there were
another kind of
language,
of love

## The Light Water Carries

*to be in an environment*
*that is always changing,*
*water moving up and down,*
*sky, light shifting*
*daily—in Gloucester*

> luminous
> translucent
> transparent
> shimmering

the flickering light on the ceiling
of the boathouse-turned studio,
tides' turning
beneath the building
light that
is also time,
moving
restlessly
across the water

through the day,
light
passes over buildings,
casting triangles of illumination
through skylights,
arms of light move across floors.

light moves over water,
playful,
flickering,
a firefly's
reflection

in this hamlet—
glowing conversation
between people
leaps from face to face
like firelight
passes
to the heart, where
thoughts linger—
a peninsula
of people,
houses like barnacles
stuck to a side of a boat

coiled ropes of light
move and cast
themselves as
pools of color on the wall—
boat shimmers;
strings of somatic language,
passages through,
connections.

a street ending in boat yards
and docks, odd buildings jumbled
together
along the way,
small alleyways,
businesses,
tiny stores
galleries,
bars, restaurants,
ebb and flow of
visitors

light spinning on top
of waves, tossing
incandescent shapes
onto floors,
ceilings

on the hill,
on the side of coves and
above studios—
following a road to the end
where it says
'Private, Visitors Welcome'
old paint factory,
now an ocean institute
    big rocks
disappearing in the tide,
lichen-covered
dry rock faces,
sumac on the other side,
dirt road you
only find if you're not looking.

And now home, in snow,
ice moves from
the sides of the river
silent
while below, water
rushes through the
channel—
near the garden
land flattens out and
the river grows quiet again—

winter with its tendrils
of snow
spiraling out of the sky
in spines of cold,
steeps us in its chill
until we have all gone inside.

—vast
unfurling it releases,
in the sky
and in ourselves:

the brave, bright light
is everywhere

## Snow Zen

snow bound
white angles
trees leaning
longer
white temples
everything
a temple
no it
no desire
no path
in the
frozen woods
no tracks
no mark
orange leaves
clustered on
frozen
trees
no
sense
nonsense,
everything,
anything
is
snow

## April

1.
In April
we walked up to
　the notch,
snow deep as
　winter
light ice flaking
　trees,
dancing lightness,
gold birches bending
　this way and
that　　a sense of possibility
　in the air
boots balancing
　on packed snow,
then sinking in deep
as we approached the
　ridge,
sun's angle divergent
　we turn
around before the notch
　itself,
three in a row,
the spring coming

2.
Remembering the hard
winter snow every day
dark skies for
New England thought
it would never end
subzero temperatures
vast amounts of snow

piling in the east
we drove there several
   times—
walked between
   walls of ice
tunnels
   idiosyncratically
shoveled for maximum
   use everyone paying
top dollar for roofs
   shoveled—
whole neighborhoods
   coming out to
chip ice off the streets
when plows couldn't
   get through
wending our way
   back to the small
valley
   where we live,
inching over the lip of
   the mountain,
waiting out the
   cold


3.
then sunlight

# Raga

lightening sky
above
brick buildings,
like
bleeding cloth,
   the dark runs out
bare trees lightly standing,
snow turning pink,
then blue-white.

like blueing on crystal gardens,
turning miniature rocks to
other-worldly wildness

bright flowers
bloom
on the windowsill,
large red buds
sweet, white
clusters of narcissus;
geraniums
crescendo
to the light


*raga: Indian musical form, literally, the act of dyeing;*
*metaphorically, expressing feeling or passion*

## May, Ocean

I stayed out long enough
to see the tide go out, and then
come in
the boat, beached, then the water lifts it,
as the brown mud flats, reflecting
sky in patches,
filled with blue.
Sky, water, low reflecting flats,
all the same color at times
and the wind picking up,
whitecaps marking the surface.

No 'I' but what was there
all around me,
rocks, crows, distant scrub on the
far beach—
tide in, tide out
with the breath

## July Études: Indemnity
*(to guard or secure against anticipated loss)*

1.
going back to a place you knew,
over long green fields,
banks of daylilies leaning toward the road,
sunlight pouring
over the lake, small houses.
your love has become part of the place itself:
sunlight
old streets
no longer hold your name
barely your memory.

2.
July rumbles thunder,
bees over the echinacea plant,
monarchs opening—closing their wings,
smell of thyme,
early rain

3.
*being the bank of lilies on*
*the hillside*
*the bird with the orange throat and chest*
*being the green hill mottled with blue shade,*
*horse chestnut tree with cones of blossom,*
*hedge of lavender.*
*rainstorm in the evening,*
*path into the deep woods.*

4.
down into the purple glade,
flowers strewn about,
gazing at the water,
   your eyes.
   clear blue—

crow cries,
water tumbles furiously
over the rock

5.
other meanings
besides the surface one,
a way in,
a handle like the red flowers over
there,
beckoning

6.
those blue eyes, more like your father's -
by the side of this water,
gooseberries
crow cries, vines
tumbling into the water below

7.
*be aware of the kinds of colors*
   *you choose,*
*are they bright—or all in one family,*
   *monochrome or contrasting?*
*colors a way in—beyond*
   *meaning—to a place that is all*
   *feeling*

8.
I read your poems with such raptness today
it was as if you were in the room
you lived two generations ago
whom I only met once
why wasn't there a woman in my
family, I wondered, who showed this
strength and emotional sureness?
and then, suddenly, there was—
she was there all along,
writing poetry
more a muse than I'd realized.

9.
What makes us feel lost for a moment,
and yet intact—
direction, a way forward
we may lose ourselves some more,
then be found
but what if we don't discover our way,
staring into the white lilies and gooseberries
forever

10.
finding  muses
who support us
through colors of like kind,
bright, in one family:
those blue eyes,
through the generations
way in,
beyond the channel of water
all the wonder
of loss

## Garden of the Hesperides


the state of mind I was in,
the golden apples had been stolen
from the corner of the yard,
the apple trees where they grew
    Hera's orchard,
where immortality was granted,
childhood never lost.
    smell of beach
roses on the wind
    trees
cicadaing in the
    August heat;
veiled horizons,
    leaves radiant,
falling asleep
    to the sound of rustling:
the one stealing the apples?

golden
apples
fallen
by a deep purple
bush,
clouds skudding over
blue sky.
bearing flowers and fruit
    at the same time,
your love
    a heartbeat
beneath
the yellow
apples

## Sailboat 1

that is me
the sailboat on the sea
the turquoise,
milky blue,
teal colored sea
sailing right by the moon,
half baked in the
cobalt sky
simplicity
one sail or two
blue on blue


## Sailboat 2

a triangle on a line
the sailboat
on the sea
shore a
diagonal
we pay for
when walking
one leg up
one down
crushed shell
grey powder
beneath our feet

## Man in Lime Colored Suit

hobbling at tide line
looking out for his feet
gingerly
balancing, arms held out
(life then and life now)
while
the girl in the spangled
turquoise bikini
picks shells
with an orange bucket
in one hand

**Friends**


peach colored dawn
behind palm fronds
wind whipping leaves
into patterns
known and unknown
    the way a strip of pink
appears, then a ribbon
    of blue
the way light glazes
    the branches


*

both became more open,
telling me things
unexpectedly
as if
I had asked,
or passed a ragged
line of trust, ribbon
of dawn behind palm
a remembered light
made real
moving fronds
in early
morning

## Cabbage

a huge surprise in the last
farmer's market of the season
gigantic cabbage,
almost more than I can hold,
walking away in my arms,
heavy and round as a bowl
for weeks
it sits on the stool
in my studio
drying up
inside
while intricate, drawn lines
emerge
on paper

one day new leaves
appear
from scars
on the thick stem,
small,
bright green curls
lift
where once huge arms
curved
outward
in the sunlight

something to draw
when the river turns white,
the weather,
cold

in Gloucester,
daily
I walked out
to draw
rocks,
the alive
line
inscribing
hard and soft edges
of boulders,
pebbles
lining the
shore

beyond my windows,
now,
the falling snow
shoots of cabbage,
ideas
on the walls

love
starts things
and
ends them—

the cabbage,
upside down,
becomes a tree

you sit beside me,
unexpectedly

**Success**


is a soft orange
peach
I hold in my hand.
it is life, life itself—
I see how it is both
something I eat,
and aspire to

the peach, all over the world,
an honored fruit.

my time,
in the orchard

## After the Paradisal Age

so we will make our kitchen
like a temple in the land of peacocks,
with green tiles that look
like feathers, adding to the
green that is already there—

why are we always making temples?
our minds, our bodies
temples—of air, of earth.
all the same, the old temples
still exist, but do the gods?

the paradisal age all but here again,
in the kitchen.

## Mountain

I sit with a view
of both river and garden,
iconically.
the columbine planted
and the iris
in bloom,
the wild rose bush
holding its own.

a lilac has escaped,
found a place in the raised
bed. at the far end I glimpse
a piece of the mountain,
blue and green, filling the space
between trees and building.

mountain, orient to our lives—
changing face daily,
silent, unnamed force
in our dreams,
spirit.
a power we all hope
to become.

Sarah Sutro's poetry is published in numerous magazines and books, including *Amsterdam Quarterly, Rockhurst Review, The Big Chili (Bangkok)*, the anthologies *Bangkok Blondes; Unbearable Uncertainty; Life Stories; Bangkok, Boston, Brattleboro: Alien Pens on Familiar Places (chapbook); Die Brucke #9*; and *The Ithaca Women's Anthology*. Author of a book of essays, *COLORS Passages through Art, Asia and Nature*, Sutro has been a finalist for the Robert Frost Award, Mass. Artists Foundation Poetry Grant, NEA and had fellowships at the MacDowell Colony, Blue Mountain Center, Millay Colony, Ossabaw Island Foundation, Arts Dulcinium in Montnegro, and the American Academy in Rome. She currently works as an editor, and writes for *American Arts Quarterly*. Her paintings can be seen at www.sarahsutro.com.